The Unexplained

The Bermuda Triangle

by Aaron Rudolph

Consultant:
Gian J. Quasar
Bermuda Triangle researcher
www.bermuda-triangle.org

Capstone
press

Mankato, Minnesota

Edge Books are published by Capstone Press
151 Good Counsel Drive, P.O. Box 669, Mankato, Minnesota 56002
www.capstonepress.com

Library of Congress Cataloging-in-Publication Data
Rudolph, Aaron.
    The Bermuda Triangle / by Aaron Rudolph.
    p. cm.—(Edge books. The unexplained)
    Includes bibliographical references and index.
    Contents: The Bermuda Triangle mystery—Lost and abandoned ships—Lost and unusual flights—Looking for answers.
    ISBN 0-7368-2718-8 (hardcover)
    1. Bermuda Triangle—Juvenile literature. [1. Bermuda Triangle.] I. Title. II. Series.
G558.R84 2005
001.94—dc22   2003024293

Editorial Credits

Carrie A. Braulick, editor; Juliette Peters, designer; Kelly Garvin, photo researcher;
    Eric Kudalis, product planning editor

Photo Credits

Bruce Coleman Inc./Andrei Sourakov, 25; Donna Rona, 26
Corbis/Bettmann, 9, 11, 14; George Hall, 20; Horace Bristol, 17; Museum of
    Flight, 19
Fortean Picture Library/Dezso Sternoczky/SUFOI, 29
Getty Images/Hulton Archive, 8
Jeff Rotman, 28
Maine Maritime Museum, 5
Michael Patrick O'Neill, cover
National Archives (NARA), 13
Naval Historic Foundation, 12
Photo Courtesy of Bruce Gernon, 22, 23

1 2 3 4 5 6 09 08 07 06 05 04

Table of Contents

FEATURES

Chapter 1

The Bermuda Triangle Mystery

In late August 1920, 11 ship crew members prepared for a long voyage. They planned to sail the *Carroll A. Deering* from Maine to South America. The ship carried a load of coal. By January 1921, the ship was returning to Maine. On January 9, the ship stopped at the island of Barbados in the Caribbean Sea.

On January 31, crew members of another ship found the *Carroll A. Deering* floating off North Carolina's coast. Its crew had vanished.

Learn about:
- *Carroll A. Deering*
- Location of the Bermuda Triangle
- Christopher Columbus' journey

The *Carroll A. Deering* was built to carry large amounts of cargo.

The ship left few clues to help others find out what happened. Food had been prepared for the crew's next meal. Crews from other ships had not heard a radio call for help from the *Carroll A. Deering*.

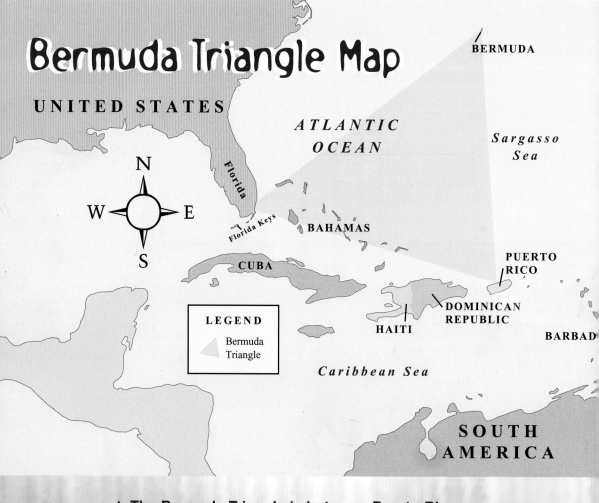

Bermuda Triangle Map

UNITED STATES

ATLANTIC OCEAN

Sargasso Sea

BERMUDA

Florida

N
W E
S

Florida Keys

BAHAMAS

CUBA

PUERTO RICO

LEGEND
Bermuda Triangle

HAITI

DOMINICAN REPUBLIC

BARBAD

Caribbean Sea

SOUTH AMERICA

▲ The Bermuda Triangle is between Puerto Rico, Bermuda, and the southeastern coast of Florida.

After the crew's disappearance, U.S. government officials investigated. They found no evidence to explain what happened.

Today, many people still wonder what happened to the crew. Some people believe the crew was captured by pirates. Other people think the crew left the ship because equipment broke. The disappearance of *Carroll A. Deering*'s crew is one of many mysteries of the Bermuda Triangle.

About the Triangle

The Bermuda Triangle lies in the Atlantic Ocean between the southeastern coast of Florida and the islands of Puerto Rico and Bermuda. An imaginary line connecting these three places forms a triangle. The Triangle covers about 500,000 square miles (1,295,000 square kilometers). It is about twice the size of Texas.

The Bermuda Triangle is one of the most mysterious places in the world. Hundreds of airplanes, ships, and boats have disappeared in the Triangle. Many ship crews and pilots have reported strange happenings in the area.

Christopher Columbus reported strange events in the Bermuda Triangle.

The Start of a Legend

One of the first reports of odd happenings in the Bermuda Triangle occurred in 1492. Christopher Columbus and his crew sailed in the Bermuda Triangle on their way to North America. Columbus reported that his compass showed unusual readings in the Sargasso Sea. The western part of the sea is in the Bermuda Triangle. Columbus' crew also noticed a light in the sky.

After Columbus' journey, other sailors told stories about the Bermuda Triangle. Stories about the Triangle continue today.

EDGE FACT

▲ The Bermuda Triangle is named for the island of Bermuda. The island forms a point of the Triangle.

Chapter 2

Lost and Abandoned Ships

Disappearances of large ships in the Bermuda Triangle were common in the 1800s and early 1900s. Some ship crews also disappeared.

Atalanta

In 1880, the British ship *Atalanta* began a journey from Bermuda to England. About 300 people were aboard. The ship failed to reach England. Rescue crews searched for it. No trace of the ship or its crew was ever found.

Learn about:
- The USS *Cyclops*
- Ship disappearances
- Missing crew members

Ships continue to disappear
in the Bermuda Triangle.

Several people suggested reasons why the ship was not found. Many people thought a storm or a crash with an iceberg caused the *Atalanta* to sink. Other people thought *Atalanta* disappeared in another part of the ocean.

▲ *Cyclops* was the largest navy ship ever to disappear leaving no clues behind.

Cyclops

In March 1918, the American military ship USS *Cyclops* disappeared in the Bermuda Triangle. The 542-foot (165-meter) navy ship was traveling from the island of Barbados near South America to Baltimore, Maryland. *Cyclops* carried more than 300 people.

▼ *Cyclops* captain George W. Worley was an experienced sailor.

Many people suggested reasons for the disappearance. Some stories said a weapon from a German submarine hit the *Cyclops*. At the time, the United States was fighting Germany and other countries in World War I (1914–1918). Another story said the ship's captain sailed to Germany and gave up the crew to the Germans. The navy proved that this story was not true. The story of the *Cyclops* remains a mystery.

EDGE FACT

▲ U.S. Coast Guard members examined the items found from the *Marine Sulphur Queen*.

Marine Sulphur Queen

In 1963, the *Marine Sulphur Queen* left Texas. The 504-foot (155-meter) ship was traveling to Maryland. Thirty-nine people were aboard. After the ship failed to arrive in Maryland, search crews looked for it. They did not find any clues. About a week later, search crews stopped looking for the ship.

Later, items from the ship were found near Key West, Florida. The items included life jackets, a fog horn, and part of a sign showing most of the ship's name. Search crews looked for a sunken ship in the area. They did not find the *Marine Sulphur Queen*.

Sylvia L. Ossa

In 1976, the 590-foot (180-meter) ship *Sylvia L. Ossa* left Brazil in South America. It was on its way to Pennsylvania. West of Bermuda, the ship's crew reported strong winds. The ship never arrived in Pennsylvania.

Search crews looked for the *Sylvia L. Ossa*. They found no clues. *Sylvia L. Ossa* was the largest ship ever to disappear in the Triangle.

Chapter 3

Lost and Unusual Flights

Ship stories are not the only Bermuda Triangle legends. Airplanes also vanish in the area. Pilots often report equipment problems in the Triangle. Electrical equipment and compasses sometimes fail.

Flight 19

One of the most famous aircraft disappearances in the Bermuda Triangle happened in 1945. On December 5, the U.S. Navy began a training exercise called Flight 19. Lieutenant Charles Taylor was the group's leader. Five pilots in Avenger torpedo bombers left Fort Lauderdale Naval Air Station in Florida.

Learn about:
• Equipment failures
• Plane disappearances
• Strange fog and lights

The pilots of Flight 19 flew
Avenger bombers.

After about two hours, Taylor called the Fort Lauderdale air base. He said he was lost. His compass had failed. The pilots were supposed to fly over the Bahama Islands, east of Fort Lauderdale. Taylor believed the group was flying over the Florida Keys, south of Florida. Air traffic controllers tried to guide the pilots back on course. But the pilots' radio messages could not be heard clearly.

About three hours later, the base lost contact with the pilots. Rescue planes were sent after the group. One of the rescue planes also disappeared. No wreckage from the five Avengers or the rescue plane was ever found.

Many people have investigated Flight 19. U.S. Navy officials said they did not know what happened to the planes. Some people think a sudden storm occurred. Some of the search pilots believe they should have been searching for wreckage farther north.

Today, researchers still want to solve the case of Flight 19. They use underwater cameras and deep diving equipment to look for wreckage.

The Lost Martin Mariner

The navy sent Martin Mariner rescue planes to find the pilots of Flight 19. Martin Mariners were sometimes called flying boats. The large planes could land on water. One of the Martin Mariners sent after Flight 19 disappeared about 20 minutes after it took off. At about the same time, ship crews in the area reported an explosion in the sky about 100 feet (30 meters) high. One ship crew noticed that a plane had disappeared from the radar screen. The other search planes came to the area to look for wreckage. None was found.

EDGE FACT

By 1940, the DC-3 was the most popular passenger plane in the world.

▲ The DC-3 can carry about 30 passengers.

The Disappearing DC-3s

In December 1948, pilot Bob Linquist was flying a DC-3 airplane over the Bermuda Triangle. The plane carried 31 passengers. Linquist planned to land at the Miami airport in Florida. He told the air traffic controllers that he was approaching the runway. But he was never heard from again. Nobody claimed to see or hear an explosion. No wreckage was ever found.

In 1978, another DC-3 airplane disappeared in the Bermuda Triangle. It was flying from Fort Lauderdale to Havana, Cuba. Pilot George Hamilton, his wife, and two other passengers were on the plane. The plane completed about half of the distance to Cuba. Then air traffic controllers noticed the plane had suddenly disappeared from their screens. Search crews never found the DC-3.

Unusual Occurrences

Many pilots have noticed strange events while flying over the Bermuda Triangle. In December 1970, pilot Bruce Gernon, his father, and a friend flew over the Triangle. Shortly after they took off, Gernon flew through a strange dark cloud. Bright flashes lit up the inside of the cloud. The plane's flight instruments failed.

▼ As Bruce Gernon flew through the cloud, the opening got smaller.

▲ **Bruce Gernon stands by his plane.**

After about 30 minutes, a tunnel-like opening appeared in the cloud. The opening began shrinking. Gernon flew toward it. He flew through the opening before it closed. Gernon and his passengers were never able to explain the cloud or the problems they experienced.

On July 11, 1986, pilot Martin Caidin and his wife had an unusual flight over the Triangle. When Caidin began the flight, the sky was clear. Then the plane flew into a yellow fog. The plane's compass and other instruments failed. Suddenly, the sky became clear again. Caidin was never able to explain the fog or why it appeared.

Chapter 4

Looking for Answers

Researchers try to explain the events in the Bermuda Triangle. They study each case to find a cause. They also try to find a common cause for the events.

Weather

Many people think that weather causes some odd events in the Triangle. Weather in the area can change quickly. Clouds can make it hard for pilots and ship crews to see. Rain and thick clouds can affect instruments on ships and planes. High winds blowing from opposite directions can destroy small planes.

Learn about:
• Bermuda Triangle storms
• Waterspouts
• Magnetic forces

Researchers believe storms may have sunk some ships in the Bermuda Triangle.

⬆ **Waterspouts can be dangerous for small ships and planes.**

Weather conditions also can cause waterspouts. These swirling winds cause sprays of water to move up from the ocean. Waterspouts can destroy small planes or ships.

Ocean Features

Natural ocean occurrences can cause some ships to sink. Areas of swirling water called whirlpools can sink small ships. Underwater earthquakes occur in the ocean. Some people think that these sudden earthquakes cause large waves. They believe the waves can cause ships to fill with water and sink.

Ocean scientist Dr. Hans Grabber believes rogue waves may cause some ships to sink. These sudden waves don't travel in groups. They are higher than other waves. Some reports say rogue waves can reach 100 feet (30 meters) high.

The makeup of the ocean can be a reason why sunken wreckage can't be found. Strong ocean currents can sweep away wreckage. The ocean floor also has areas of quicksand and deep trenches. Ships and airplanes that fall into quicksand or trenches can be hard to find.

▼ **Trenches can make some sunken ships hard to find.**

Other Theories

People have suggested other theories. The U.S. Navy believes human error causes most Bermuda Triangle disappearances. They believe pilots and captains misjudge their location. Some researchers say mines left behind from times of war sank some ships.

Scientist John Hutchinson believes magnetic forces may exist in the Triangle. He believes the magnetic forces can cause equipment failures, green lights, or fog.

An Ongoing Legend

Many well-known disappearances in the Triangle happened more than 30 years ago. Today, better equipment helps captains and pilots stay on course and communicate.

But planes and ships continue to disappear. Since the late 1970s, more than 75 aircraft and 1,000 boats have disappeared in the Triangle.

The Bermuda Triangle has interested people for hundreds of years. People continue to wonder what causes the disappearances and strange events there.

The Devil's Sea

Japanese sailors call the water off the southeastern coast of Japan the Devil's Sea. The area is part of the Pacific Ocean. Sailors tell stories about the Devil's Sea that are similar to Bermuda Triangle stories. Some scientists believe the Devil's Sea has magnetic fields similar to the Bermuda Triangle. They think the magnetic fields could cause the odd events.

Glossary

compass (KUHM-puhss)—an instrument people use to find the direction in which they are traveling; a compass has a needle that points north.

iceberg (EYESS-berg)—a huge piece of ice that floats in the ocean; icebergs break off from glaciers.

pirate (PYE-rit)—a person who attacks and steals from ships at sea

quicksand (KWIK-sand)—loose, wet sand that can trap objects

trench (TRENCH)—a long, narrow steep-sided hole in the ocean floor

waterspout (WAW-tur-spowt)—a mass of spinning cloud-filled wind that stretches from a cloud to a body of water; waterspouts force up a strong spray of water in lakes and oceans.

whirlpool (WURL-pool)—a water current that moves rapidly in a circle; ships and boats can become caught in whirlpools.

Read More

Donkin, Andrew. *Bermuda Triangle.* Eyewitness Readers. New York: DK Publishing, 2000.

Gorman, Jacqueline Laks. *The Bermuda Triangle.* X Science. Milwaukee: Gareth Stevens, 2002.

Innes, Brian. *The Bermuda Triangle.* Unsolved Mysteries. Austin, Texas: Raintree Steck-Vaughn, 1999.

Rosenberg, Aaron. *The Bermuda Triangle.* Unsolved Mysteries. New York: Rosen, 2002.

Internet Sites

FactHound offers a safe, fun way to find Internet sites related to this book. All of the sites on FactHound have been researched by our staff.

Here's how:
1. Visit *www.facthound.com*
2. Type in this special code **0736827188** for age-appropriate sites. Or enter a search word related to this book for a more general search.
3. Click on the **Fetch It** button.

FactHound will fetch the best sites for you!

Index